GET OUT OF YOUR OWN WAY

*20 Secrets to Stop Being the Biggest
Obstacle to Living the Life You Choose*

*10 Ways to Tap into Your Subconscious
and Get the Universe on Your Side*

KAREN LEEDS
Life Coaching Magic

Karen Leeds, Life Coaching Magic

"You are amazing and insightful!"

"I feel relaxed and in control of my life."

"I am thinking about my life in a new way."

www.LifeCoachingMagic.com

ISBN: 978-0-9969069-1-3

GET YOUR FREE EBOOK AT

www.LifeCoachingMagic.com

(for a little life coaching magic)

"STOP SWABBING SOMEONE ELSE'S DECK AND CAPTAIN YOUR OWN SHIP!"

Karen Leeds
Life Coach

Dedicated to my son and daughter - the most amazing kids (okay - they are now adults) that a person could have. I love you both and am so grateful to have you in my life. And I am glad that you are always happy to encourage me in learning how to get out of my own way so that I can pass that along to others.

CONTENTS

10 ways to tap into your subconscious and the universe:

ACKNOWLEDGMENTS

I realize I am so glad that I put on the last page of my first book that I would publish this book by January 2023.

If I hadn't done that I'm not sure it would have happened.

So I just wanted to say thanks to whoever decided that deadlines are important. They really knew what they had stumbled upon!

Thanks to all the people who bought and gave feedback on my first book since it encouraged me to keep writing.

Here are those who were essential to this book:

Jon Fischer at JonFischerPhotography.com - cover photo

Lisa Alpert at WebThreeSixty.com - creating book cover as well as website support

Donna Kozik at Done for You Publishing - publishing assistance

Shannon Rasmussen - book editing

ABOUT THE AUTHOR

Karen Leeds, founder of Life Coaching Magic, enjoys making a huge difference in 1:1 coaching with clients. Karen has studied personal growth since she was 14, and while she finds coaching rewarding, she decided it would be helpful to reach a broader audience, making a greater impact on people's happiness and success.

Karen's other books:

- "Life's Magic Carousel: How to Grab the Brass Ring Before the Music Stops" has fun quotes and illustrations and earned great feedback that it was powerful, fun, and easy to read.

- "Speak So People Hear You" includes crazy true stories and was published in January 2023.

She has written 13 articles for GoodMenProject.com. These articles can be discovered by typing in KAREN LEEDS.

Karen is featured in BostonVoyager.com, an online magazine that profiles local business owners. The article can be viewed by typing in KAREN LEEDS.

Karen has also published several short stories:

- "My Fearless Five-Year-Old Self" in a collection of 42 short stories called "If Only I Knew Then What I Know Now." (Karen feels like she has spent the rest of her life trying to get back to who she was at age 5.)

- "My Suddenly Grateful Self" in a collection called "I Can Feel the Love." (It was inspired by both the Andover/North Lawrence gas explosions and Karen's parents' deaths 4 months apart. Karen discovered there is always a silver lining in whatever happens.)

- "Ferret Shenanigans or Simply Odd?" in Donna Kozik's collection of stories called "Pawsome Friends." (It is about Karen's daughter's ferret, Georgie -- possibly an oddball, though he was the only ferret she has known.)

- "One Incredibly Free-Wheeling Woman" in Donna Kozik's collection of stories titled "The Gratitude Book Project." (Karen discovered that she had freedom once there was no longer a boyfriend, child or pet at home.)

INTRODUCTION

I realized that there are so many things that would have been helpful if we had learned them when we were young and impressionable. (Wouldn't it be great if these were taught in school?)

But since that didn't happen I decided to turn one of my workshop presentations into this book. So this is my second offering - somewhat of a "life coach in a book."

You may notice that I have a sense of humor. (It is getting much harder to hide that as I lose inhibitions I've had for decades.) Over the years, I have discovered that people learn better when they are relaxed and smiling, so I am sneaky and offer teaching when folks have their guard down. It helps both of us!

Enjoy these 30 secrets so that you, too, can get out of your own way. I suspect you will discover as I have that life is suddenly easier, as well as more fun and rewarding.

Having illustrations made for my first book took a lot of time and energy. I was wondering what I might do instead, when it occurred to me. I've been writing poetry since I was 5 years old. So I decided to write a poem for each of the secrets I outline. I haven't had such fun in ages! (I actually wrote these 30 poems in two days, but don't tell anyone; I'd hate for that to get out.)

20 SECRETS TO STOP BEING THE BIGGEST OBSTACLE TO LIVING THE LIFE YOU CHOOSE

SECRET #1: YOU

YOU = **Y**ou
         Only
              Understand

(Hey, if you don't understand then we're in trouble here.)

Others may believe they know what we should do, but that isn't always the case. They aren't sitting in our shoes - or if they are - it might be good to ask why? (If their shoes are uncomfortable maybe they should get new ones.)

It is definitely best to believe in yourself and trust your decisions. (Later I'll talk specifically about how to more easily make decisions - we were taught one way to do it but there is a way that definitely brings us greater happiness and peace of mind.)

The best thing about us is that we are human beings, not robots. Sure, that can lead to difficulty at times since we might make mistakes or do things that we later understand weren't in our best interests. But it is okay if we aren't just going to plod along in a boring straight line. In fact, deciding to get away from the traditional route can often be what gives us the most satisfaction.

As a strong introvert I prefer giving talks to small groups, so my presenting at a local library is a fit. My deciding to give a TEDx talk? Maybe, but don't hold your breath.

Why is it that I've dimmed my light?
Tried to fit in - but that's not right.

I get to be me, in all my glory
Not hiding from my honest story.

It's time for me to shine and glow
Allow others to get to know

Just what I offer here and now
And maybe they might just say "Wow

This person that I thought I knew
I honestly just had no clue."

They might begin to really see
Just what it is that makes me, me.

So stop trying to be someone you're not
And shine your bright 1000 watt!

- Karen Leeds

SECRET #2: TRUE STRENGTH AND BRAVERY

(Hey - don't chicken out on me now.)

Having it all = **HAVE**

    Honest

        Authentic

            Vulnerable

                Enjoying Life

Be unapologetically you. We often feel bad that we aren't like others. Hey, let's give that up, okay?

I'm here to tell you that you are great just as you are!

We are all different and that is often a good thing. How boring would the world be if we were all identical?

What if you just appreciate those qualities that make you unique? (I realize this might be a radical idea.)

Sometimes we feel that we have to be dishonest and cover up who we really are. But true strength and bravery actually come from showing up with courage - being vulnerable and authentic.

Picture how much easier it would feel to be yourself instead of spending so much energy and effort masquerading as something or someone you aren't? Like being a spy (ooh that sounds like fun - at least briefly).

Most of us try to be what we are not, covering up our true essence. It is important instead to tune in and be authentically yourself - and frankly it is much easier. The sense of freedom can be incredible!

Let's say that as a student you were nervous about raising your hand in class. After all, what would people think of you? But suppose others had the same question. In that case, you'd actually be doing them a favor, helping them understand as well. And you'd then know the answer. Clearly a win/win.

Frankly I am quirky, silly, funny, caring and definitely imperfect. For years I tried to hide my true self. But now I'm fully embracing my uniqueness. And I've discovered that people respond well to it. I suggest you might want to consider doing the same thing.

It is wonderful to be able to relax and truly enjoy life when we can breathe again. Try it sometime!

So if you've pretended that you love art museums or that you're happy in your job or that you don't mind listening to someone in your life complain, maybe it's time to pay attention to the gap between what you're doing or who you are being and what you are really all about.

Having it all sounds really good
As it definitely and undeniably should.
We get to live the way that's right
For us - during both day and night.

No longer do our parents choose
If so, it often seems we lose
That fragile important sense of self
We sometimes put up on a shelf.

It's time to be the one we are
And we don't have to be a star.
Except in our own life of course
On carousel, astride our chosen horse.

- Karen Leeds

[Note: This page was going to be intentionally left blank but then I discovered that I couldn't leave it that way without some sort of explanation. I didn't want people to worry that somehow a page wasn't printed. Oh, the horror!

I might be a bit OCD but I sort of liked the idea of each secret being on the left-hand page with the associated poem on the right-hand page. It has a nice, consistent, orderly, rhythmic feel to it.

But then I ended up with a blank page - hence this somewhat lengthy explanation.

The good news is that years ago I would have worried about it. Now, instead, I do something about it; likely completely unnecessary but this is what I'm about - sometimes overexplaining.

Have I suggested yet that I studied personal growth for decades because I needed to learn how to get out of my own way?

In any case, there you have it - a simple explanation with much more detail than necessary.

I hope that you are feeling reassured and can now get back to reading about Secret #3 which ironically is "Stop Trying to Be Perfect." Hope the coincidence isn't lost on you, my faithful, patient audience.]

SECRET #3: STOP TRYING TO BE PERFECT

(Hey, I'm keeping my eye on you.)

We are human - and that's really okay. (The dinosaurs are no longer around, right? Guess that tells you something.)

We are allowed to be imperfect - truly!

We tend to twist ourselves into pretzels in our relationships: at work, with relatives, with friends or even in significant relationships. We try to do everything and anything to be perfect in that role. Seriously - why? That doesn't actually make you happy and, surprisingly, it often doesn't make the other person happy either. Once we are stressed and fall short of perfection, we go on to beat ourselves up about it.

What if you take a pledge right now:

I PROMISE TO LET GO OF TRYING TO BE PERFECT

(Hey - this is in bold so you can't ignore it)

If you don't feel comfortable saying that, maybe think about trying it on and consider how it might feel? (Good, right?) It can be exciting to give up impossible standards that we have been attempting to meet for years. (Hmmm - was that really working well for you anyway?)

If you can't let go yet, I promise that I will hold space for you to do so. Now just relax and breathe.

Perfection, bah humbug, is over-rated
And striving for it sure seems outdated.

We do our best - hey that's enough
Though our end results might be quite rough.

Congratulate ourselves for our attempt
Even if from struggle we may not be exempt.

Our wins we applaud - yes, we can do it
Lower that bar and we'll soar over it.

Just think how awesome - what a thrill
When we've done our best - then we can chill.

- Karen Leeds

SECRET #4: THE MAGIC OF POSSIBILITY

(Wait. I've got my magic wand somewhere. Hang on.)

It sounds silly but it turns out that if we believe in possibility then good things actually happen.

I met someone who was going for a job interview. They said that getting a job was hard, but just picture how they would show up if they believed that. Their defeated body language would be obvious to the person doing the interviewing if they were slumped and looking dejected. How likely would it be that they would be hired in that case?

You might think that you are deceiving yourself, but frankly many people get jobs. Hey, you can choose to believe that you can have what you want. And I guarantee that the interviewer will respond more positively.

So think of one thing you want. (Now that's the way. I bet you are smiling while you are doing so.)

One day I was thinking how nice it would be if I got to spend more time with a dog I thoroughly enjoy. The next day her owner asked if I could take her for a weekend! I don't know if that might have happened anyway, but I can't help but believe that my putting out that wish helped make it happen. (And I didn't even wave my magic wand about it.)

What is possible? Let's look and see.
Whatever we want - hey, that's for me!*

It feels so good to imagine it's there
From here I can get anywhere.

Whatever I want, when I believe
It seems then I can truly conceive

I create it now, hey there it is
The universe provides, so right that is.

The world is really on my side
Supporting my wishes - it turns the tide.

I know that in my heart it's true
Not just for me, but also for you!

- Karen Leeds

*Debra Poneman of Yes to Success suggested that it is empowering to say "And that's for me."

SECRET #5: TUNE IN TO WHAT YOU WANT

(That's right - what YOU want. Hey, I'm not a mind reader.)

What you want matters - a lot!

Sometimes we are focused on others and what they want, but denying yourself doesn't usually have a good outcome. At some point, you feel cheated. (And we broadcast that clearly.)

Just picture: Wouldn't it be great if you had no regrets at the end of your life?

We tend to do what we think we SHOULD be doing. But that rarely helps us achieve happiness or peace.

When we get quiet and pay attention to what we really want we can go after that. Not in a selfish way (knocking others to the ground) but in a way that makes us feel whole and nurtured.

In fact, giving to others (when we choose to do so) can be rewarding. (I return people's grocery carts because they feel seen and I love giving back. Once I helped a woman with a cane unload stuff and we both cried happy tears.)

What are things that feed your soul? Is it people, activities, places, animals, or nature? (I'll never forget going to a COSTUME DANCE with my BOYFRIEND. It was crazy; not just one but three things I enjoyed - all at once too!)

What do you want in your heart of hearts?
Stop living life in fits and starts.

Go after things that make you grow
Take on that crazy afterglow.

The people you see, the things you do
How you give back to this world, too.

So often we forget our heart
Then wishes and actions seem miles apart.

So now you get to pave the way
And live each hour of each new day

Excited to wake and raring to go
Your life will more easily ebb and flow.

- Karen Leeds

SECRET #6: DON'T THROW YOURSELF UNDER A BUS

(Don't do it; those things are big and scary!)

Stop trying to please people. (For crying out loud, it's amazing how often we do that.)

Newsflash - you get just one life!

What if you decide that what you want is important?

Yes, it's wonderful to help others. And there's a time and place for that. But if you find that you are practically doing somersaults to avoid disappointing others, that is not making a priority of you and your needs.

I had a client who never spoke up. Her mom didn't either, so they were both unhappy because they felt like they shouldn't talk about things. Once I came on the scene, they started having conversations and realized that what they were doing wasn't really working for either of them.

You are here for more!

Now if they gave points for how we could tie ourselves in knots that would be a whole different matter. But they don't. (Trust me, I finally figured this one out.)

There are things under our control. Focus on those and you might be surprised how much calmer, more centered and peaceful your life can feel.

Don't throw yourself under a bus
Then others will have to come and fuss.

Your life is worth far more than that
Stop being a statistic or forgone fact.

You get to say to what you'll commit
And others will then be respecting it.

Becoming a pretzel's an uncomfortable deal
And not at all cushy - a bunched up feel.

Let's go for something that really works
The way you want things, in the background lurks.

Bring those into the light of day
Now you can live life just your way.

- Karen Leeds

SECRET #7: CREATE MOMENTUM

(Wait - I bet you might need to get something going first.)

It is remarkable how we can avoid doing something for a long time.

What's interesting is that doing one little thing, almost anything, can have incredible results.

For example, I read a great book called "Clear Your Clutter with Feng Shui" by Karen Kingston.

The author said to set a timer for five minutes for each room. I went into my bedroom and when the timer went off, I was surprised that the five minutes went by so quickly. As it turned out, I kept resetting the timer and ended up organizing my bedroom for a whole hour! Now if someone had told me that I had to go spend an hour picking up my room I wouldn't have done it. Nope - no way.

The same thing works for trying to get healthier. If you give up all sweets at once you feel cheated. But small goals are much easier to achieve. I helped a client lose 7 pounds in 12 days. (She wanted to fit into a dress for a special occasion.) She changed very little about her routine, but little tweaks made a big difference.

What small changes might have a positive effect on the things you want to be different in your life?

No need to take a giant leap
Just take one itty-bitty creep
And then like that you'll find things move
So simple really and so smooth.

You start to see the progress then
And as you do, you'll notice when
Things in your world - they start to shift
Like an earthquake at its first big rift.

And quickly you're excited to make
One change. Although it isn't fake,
Your world is new - it's looking good
Where once your "I can't do it" stood.

And now you do believe your life
Gone are angst, the aarrgghh, the strife.
This way will work. Wow - who knew?
Well, I suppose I could say who.

It took me years to figure out
What now I'm off to shout about.
The things to do if we only try
Our world awaits with patient sigh.

- Karen Leeds

SECRET #8: DON'T TAKE REJECTION PERSONALLY

(Honestly, I didn't mean it. Jeez. Are we okay now?)

We often think that we are being rejected. We tend to assume that things are about us. It is important to get over ourselves because we are not the center of the universe. (Wait - was that a shock? I'm sorry about that.)

I had a client who would ask for a woman's phone number. Then, if she didn't respond to a text, he would take to his bed for two days.

But I asked, what if when you asked for her number, she explained that though you were a great guy, she didn't see it as a fit? In that case, he would likely have just shrugged it off and not taken it personally.

Kids of divorce often believe that the divorce is their fault. It usually isn't, but they tend to blame themselves.

Sorry to break it to you, but we are typically not nearly as important as we think we are, especially in terms of being the cause of difficult things. Take responsibility when it makes sense, but don't look to shoulder blame. Often circumstances can be complicated and there isn't a single contributing factor.

Repeat after me: THINGS AREN'T ALWAYS ABOUT ME!

Hey, that I just had not conceived
Not a rejection as I believed.

It wasn't aimed at me - gee
That arrow thrown - 'twas not aimed at me.

I made it mean something, that is true
Thought it was about me, but 'twas about you.

I understand that it's your deal
I'll leave it with you - I will not steal.

So, I will walk with my head held high
From now on I won't own the sky.

When I hear no, I will brush it away
Shake my head and get on with my day.

- Karen Leeds

SECRET #9: WHEN TO TOSS THE PLAN

(Yikes - just be careful where you toss it!)

We often hate to decide that our "plan" or what we are doing isn't working.

But sometimes it is best to toss the plan and improvise!

We get invested in something we've been working toward. But maybe it really isn't in our best interests, or in the interest of others, if it is so hard to accomplish?

I'm not talking about giving up when something is difficult or time consuming. But if what you are doing isn't rewarding it might be time to switch to something that is a fit for you.

There is often a "sunk" cost that we might not notice. We feel like we've spent time, money, and energy working toward something. But what about the emotional cost? If we are feeling discouraged and out of alignment with what we want in our lives, then it could be a clue that what we are doing isn't really working well for our best interests.

Here's a fun example of a letter that I created for a parent to send their adult child. Sometimes trying a different approach can be successful (humor is often a good choice):

Dear _____,

This is a letter from your clothes. Being here, we saw what kind of a life other clothes have.

Was it something that we did?

We are feeling pretty giddy at the moment...

We would like to come home but are wondering, could you be a little bit nicer to us?

Or release us to someone who will?

Thanks!
Your forever grateful clothes

Shifting approaches when something isn't working can often be successful.

You can then discover whether making a change brings about a positive result. If so, great. If not, you can always try a different approach. Flexibility is often a big advantage.

If things don't work, I'll stop my boot
And find a different path or route.

This plan's not working - that is true
So instead of muttering or starting to stew,

I will change tactics and you might see
A completely different side of me.

One that can shift - respond anew
As I start to see what works with you.

My focus is on the results I get
Until they're good I'm not done yet.

So, I'll be curious and try a new way
Tomorrow I'll have another say.

\- Karen Leeds

SECRET #10: BE STRONG
AND CONFIDENT

(No, you don't need to be the silent type - thank goodness. I sure couldn't.)

There are typically things we do that undermine our confidence and have an impact on others too.

We might, for example, raise our voice at the end of a sentence. It just shows uncertainty - and that's probably not something we want to project.

So if you're a boss or parent and you're giving direction, it is best not to raise your voice at the end of sentence as if it were a question (or as if you were asking for permission):

"Let's take a 15-minute break?" or "Get ready to go?"

Some often-used words tend to undermine certainty:
- "I think"
- "I believe"
- "It seems like"
- "Maybe"

Instead of saying "I think we should change our investment strategy."

You sound more confident saying:

"We should change our investment strategy."

Try it on for size - you'll feel so much more in charge.

You've got this now - you're strong you'll see
Soon you won't need to hear it from me.

You're smart and kind, decisive, too
The world has just been waiting for you.

Believe in yourself and others will see
What you hoped that there would be.

So, trust, stand tall -- you've got this now
When you speak, people think "holy cow."

Your confidence you now might find
Comes not just from dim back of mind.

But precedes you as you go through your day
In a completely different amazing way.

- Karen Leeds

SECRET #11: YOU ARE LOVED, WORTHY AND ENOUGH

(Wait… you didn't know how incredible you are?)

We often wait for others to say how wonderful we are. Unfortunately, we feel like we're not good enough unless others believe in us.

But what if you decide here and now that you are loved, worthy, and enough? Without anyone else expressing that out loud? (Sounds radical, right?)

And let's take it a step further.

What if you decide you deserve to live a great life? Now!

In fact, what if you say it out loud:

"I give myself permission to live a great life!"

And I'll go further. If you don't feel comfortable doing so, I will give you permission. Are you ready for it?

You have permission to live a great life!

There, I said it. Now it can't be undone. Nope.

Believing that you have permission to live a great life is the most important first step in building the life that you picture in your dreams. Then you are more likely to get to where you want your life to be.

We wander through our life so low
Not realizing that WE create the show.

Understand that you are quite enough
And others will see that you are tough.

It's time to know that we are a prize
To folks this shouldn't be a surprise.

They often believe it before we do
And finally, now, we'll make it true.

We'll walk along with our head held high
Thank goodness we no longer have to just try.

We've earned the right to shine it's true
Now it's much brighter than both me and you.

\- Karen Leeds

SECRET #12: THE MIND IS A SCARY PLACE

(The worst is when your shoes get stuck in the grey matter - yuck!)

We spend so much time with our thoughts.

But our mind isn't always a good place to be. (Albert Ellis called it "stinking thinking.")

In fact, there is a saying I created:

"The mind is a scary place; don't venture there alone!"

Seriously - if you find yourself stuck with your thoughts, it can be paralyzing. (Trust me - I know.) Those thoughts go around and around. And then you aren't doing anything.

The more we catch certain thoughts like worry, guilt, and should, the more peaceful our lives will be.

If you find yourself worrying - stop it. I'm serious; worry is useless. It doesn't change anything, and it consumes a whole lot of unnecessary time and energy.

Guilt is very similar: You can feel guilty - or you can decide to do something different in the future. You can even apologize (to yourself or others).

If you find that you are "shoulding" on yourself - give it up if you can. It is tricky living up to an impossible standard. Now you'll have room to breathe!

The mind is a scary place (and zone)
Don't venture in there all alone.

Your thoughts - they do block out the light
And keep us hiding through the long night.

It's time to stop giving power to thought
Like a prison for us - it is truly fraught,

With places we can get stuck for years
And find ourselves then drenched in tears.

But none of it works for our good
Even if we once thought it should.

So now we will take back our might
And say no to thoughts that aren't right.

- Karen Leeds

SECRET #13: WATCH YOUR LANGUAGE

(It can weigh heavily on you like a ton of bricks.)

There is a wonderful, empowering way to change the language you use.

Instead of saying I HAVE TO or I MUST or I NEED TO, there is an alternative.

Think how much freer you will feel if, instead, you say:

I CHOOSE TO do my taxes.

It sounds silly, but the language we use actually does make a big difference.

Or what if instead of saying "I never get things right" you say:

"I'm EXCITED about the way that I spoke up today."

Or what if instead of saying "Nobody wants to date me" you say:

"The right person will come along and APPRECIATE who I am."

Or instead of saying "Nothing goes well for me" you say:

"THAT WENT SO WELL."

Hey - watch your language - it sure does matter
"I CHOOSE TO" sounds so much better.

"I MUST, I HAVE TO, I NEED TO" all rot.
It's my choice and frankly whether or not

I work on something today and "why"
Can be empowering - so don't be shy.

You "GET TO"* - so you can count on things
That's the spirit - now go flap those wings!

\- Karen Leeds

*Mel Mason suggested that you "get to" do something

SECRET #14: LOTTERY - WHAT WOULD YOU DO IF YOU WON?

(Frankly, I'm so excited I'm skipping around!)

One day I bought a lottery ticket. And I said to myself "I hope I win."

Then I got curious about that. Hmmm, why exactly did I want to win?

And I mentioned a few things that I would want to do (in that scary mind where you're not supposed to venture alone). Curiously enough, I discovered that I didn't need to win to experience many things on my list.

- Instead of going on an expensive vacation, I could take a day trip or go to an Airbnb for a weekend.
- Instead of going on a safari, I could go to a petting zoo (less expensive and likely much safer too).
- Instead of buying an expensive outfit, I could get clothing at a reasonably priced chain store.
- Instead of spending money on costly theater, sports, or music tickets, I could find free events to attend.
- Instead of signing up for a year-long program, I could take a 6-week course.

While not quite the same they are still fulfilling!

What on earth would you do if you won?
It sounds incredible but think on that one.
Do what you choose - so what would it be?
Your imagination can run up a tree!
The world is your oyster so let it take off
You've won this now, don't let others scoff.
What is there in your heart's great desire?
We've started the kindling for this warming fire.
The reins are now held loosely in your hand
Where would you want to go in this land?
Or would you prefer to move, if so
Where might you decide you would go?
It's all up to you - you're the big boss
Don't let your dreams just sit and grow moss.
It's time to explore what you'd like to be
And that might be more than ocean or sea.
So, take some time and figure this out
Check out those maps or send out a scout.
Your dreams can't wait, it's time to enjoy
An experience - like a dog with a toy.
So, what will it be that gives you a smile?
You've been on this planet for maybe awhile
Give thought to your wishes and then you can choose
And no matter what - there's no way you'll lose.

- Karen Leeds

SECRET #15: LIVE IN THE PRESENT

(This moment right here. Hey - are you paying attention?)

We often think about the future (futurizing) or worry about what might happen (catastrophizing).

Stop that! The best thing is to be fully in the present.

We can't control the future, and we can't change the past.

BE HERE NOW, LIVE FOR NOW!

Folks often take photos and selfies, and while I enjoy them, I realize that if I spend a lot of time taking photos, it completely removes me from the moment.

I also tend to focus on people (which is fine) but I'm learning to look around. I remember one time I was with a friend who commented about the amazing décor on the walls and ceilings of the restaurant we were in. I hadn't noticed either one! I was just looking at her.

Since then, I try to occasionally look around and notice details when I am out in nature, at a party, or by myself.

It gives us more energy when we pay attention, not to mention being more fully engaged with the world.

This is also what I appreciate most about others. It is quite unusual to talk with someone who is completely present!

To live in the present -- it really sounds nice
But what does it mean as you're stirring the rice?
How is it different from how you have been?
And why will it matter now and again?

Once you're here feeling calm and we all see the change
Your thoughts aren't stormy -- your legs they don't range.
Your heart will expand so full in your chest.
You realize that all of this sure trumps the rest.

So, let the past go and stop all the worry
The future will come -- there's no need to hurry.
Your friends will appreciate when you are near
It's possible that some might even cheer.

Why wasn't this known? You discover that most
Are rarely here -- their energy's toast.
They worry and wonder and don't see the thrill
Of feeling peaceful and remarkably chill.

- Karen Leeds

SECRET #16: HOW DO YOU SPEND YOUR TIME?

(If you find yourself drooling, maybe watch fewer cooking shows.)

We spend a lot of time and energy these days on email, Facebook, TV and other things that can be a bit of a rathole for us. Then we look up and discover that time has passed rather quickly.

The most important question is whether you are spending your time in ways that you choose? Do your choices make you feel fulfilled or are you just passing the time? Would you be happier reading, spending time with a friend, volunteering, or painting?

Freeing up time can be rewarding.

What if you consider one thing that you will choose to spend less time doing?

I discovered that I was spending a huge amount of time watching the news recently. It was amazing how much time and energy I released by stopping that. Now I watch occasionally and listen to news on the radio while driving because it feels like a much better use of my time. And then I don't look around at the end of the day and wonder where my time went.

A few years ago, I found myself in 4 business groups. Seriously? They were taking up so many hours I couldn't find time for my business that I was promoting!

At the end of the day, I look around
What an odd discovery I seem to have found.

My day was quickly pulled away
By social media posts -- at my computer I'd stay.

And then wonder what I had gotten done
Who wins when I'm not having fun?

I'd rather see folks, earth, and sky
Or write or draw. I wonder why

Us humans sadly give our time
To things that sometimes make us whine.

But now I know that I do rate
Technology is not my fate!

I'll take the helm and steer this ship
Gather the reins and crack that whip.

I'll only do what now I choose
So that peace and joy I never lose.

- Karen Leeds

SECRET #17: INTERRUPTIONS

(Wait… what thought just left my head? It's sure gone now.)

Interruptions can be tricky. There you are making progress on something when you suddenly get stopped. It can be hard to pick up where you left off - or even remember where that was.

But the fact that someone interrupts you doesn't mean that you need to deal with it right then.

Sometimes viewing it as "not my crisis" or "not my timing" can be helpful.

Sure, there will be times that things are urgent and need to be dealt with immediately. But often that isn't the case.

You could ask - Can I get back to you tomorrow afternoon about this?

Life is easier when you're not giving in to things that stop you in your tracks but that may not be urgent.

(Now if you're hoping for interruptions to save you from what you're immersed in, that could require a whole different conversation about your choices.)

Ain't my worry, ain't my stuff
Stop interrupting me for fluff.

I now do me - I take a stand
I wish I'd known this but now I can

Keep my priorities front and center
And block all those who try to enter

Folks steal my time for what they want
Whether serious or for a jaunt.

My world feels brighter - I look around
My feet now firmly on the ground.

I've time to breathe and smile at last
My day no longer whizzes by so fast.

Life looks better - I love this view
Why does this now seem really new?

These things they should be taught in school
And made a life-long golden rule.

- Karen Leeds

SECRET #18: DECISION-MAKING

(Yikes - but waffling back and forth is so entertaining.)

My dad used to explain how to easily make decisions.

He said that you create a list of the pros and cons of each choice. It seemed straight forward, right?

But I discovered that sometimes even if one choice looks better on paper that doesn't mean it is the right decision for me.

Also, there is a difference between a head decision (the list of pluses and minuses) and a heart decision.

The way to make a heart decision is to get quiet, tune in to what you want - which choice really calls to you - and find what might be the best choice for you alone.

Other people might have strong ideas as to what they think works for you. But do they really know you well enough to decide for you? Don't let others pull you off center. When we were kids, parents made decisions for us that they believed were in our best interest. But as adults, we can change the way we make decisions for ourselves.

So be true to yourself - your values, your strengths, your desires and your beliefs. Though we might be good at ignoring our feelings, it can be important to actually see what those feelings are desperately trying to tell us.

I look inside and now I see
Just what is truly best for me.

Not for others - this is mine.
Be true to myself and all will be fine.

So I thank those for their advice.
It can be helpful and at times nice.

But really check in - oh there it is.
How had I missed it? Gee whiz.

What thing is best for me right now?
(The choice that gives me a strong wow.)

It feels so right - how'd I not know?
The seeds which I will now go sow.

\- Karen Leeds

SECRET #19: UP UNTIL NOW

(Sorry, buddy, but change is sometimes really good.)

There is a terrific tool that is a great way to draw a line in the sand:

UP UNTIL NOW

Your future isn't set in stone. And it doesn't need to be determined by the past - at least not anymore!

This tool releases the past and doesn't bring it forward into the future. And remember - your subconscious is always listening. So leave the door open for you to learn!

In the past, you might have believed you weren't good at holding onto money, making friends, or meditating. But:

- Instead of saying "I'm not good with money" say

"Up until now, I wasn't focused on saving money."

- Instead of saying "Nobody wants to be my friend" say

"Up until now, I felt shy making friends."

- Instead of saying "I'm not good at meditating" say

"Up until now, I wasn't sure how to meditate."

Up until now, I've put up with those
Not friends I like or ones I chose.

But here I draw a line in the sand
I put my foot down and take a stand.

It's what I want - it's me that matters
Not pleasing, with my life in tatters.

I get to do this journey my way
And not just for one single day.

So, look out folks - it might surprise
This solid look in my two eyes.

I can be strong, decisive, too,
No more do I come after you!

- Karen Leeds

SECRET #20: POWER OF POSITIVITY

(But whining and complaining can be so much fun!)

Going through life feeling happy and positive instead of sad and negative can be a terrific way to go. (I recognize that might sound odd.)

I remember hearing a story about two families in neighboring houses whose homes had been destroyed by a huge fire.

One family said they had lost everything, and they didn't know how they could possibly continue living that way.

The other family said that their house was definitely gone, but that all members of their family were still alive and that they could just rebuild. To them, the property wasn't nearly as important as their lives, and if they had each other, they could absolutely continue.

I also knew of a neighbor who would always complain that things were terrible, but it was rarely anything serious that she was personally facing. Where do you go from there if you believe that things are already terrible? What if something bad actually happens to you? It's such a sad, depressing way to live.

You will feel more peaceful and relaxed, and people will enjoy hanging out with you more, if you see the glass as half full instead of as half empty!

It seems a small thing but it's not
To look on the bright side at what you've got.

Instead of worrying about what might snap
And have that create an energy zap.

If you are often a negative Nancy
Instead see what's good - doesn't have to be fancy.

If, at first, you don't see a plus
Change your lens - don't make a fuss.

Have positivity be your default
Like characters from Disney (you know - Walt).

The world is better when we add our smile
Even when it's rusty or been awhile.

So, put your grin back on your face
It helps not just animals but the whole human race.

- Karen Leeds

10 WAYS TO TAP INTO YOUR SUBCONSCIOUS AND GET THE UNIVERSE ON YOUR SIDE

The following 10 secrets help you tap into your subconscious and the universe. Most of us are not typically aware of these other forces.

We don't realize how much of our lives are not controlled by our conscious mind since most of our education relates to our thoughts.

Surprisingly, not only is our subconscious running the show of our lives, but the universe also weighs in, depending on our energy and what we put out into the world.

For example, cancer patients fare much better if they picture themselves doing well. Those thoughts reach out to both their subconscious and the universe (and beyond).

To be more powerful we have these additional 10 secrets.

*[Note: This page was going to
intentionally be left blank as well.*

Here we go again.

*I wrestled with offering a brief explanation of the following
10 secrets. But I felt it was important to do so even though
that threw off the perfect formatting with the secret on the
left-hand page and the poem on the right-hand page. No!*

*So, I hope you are all remembering
to breathe. You've got this.*

(I'll try to remember to breathe as well.)

*May you enjoy these subconscious and other worldly
secrets, including the next one which is "Look for
the Silver Lining." The silver lining here is that I
apparently kept your attention so you didn't panic
that a page might be missing and then neglect to read
the last 10 secrets. So it looks like a win/win.]*

SECRET #21: LOOK FOR THE SILVER LINING

(I know this is new but seriously, give it a try.)

Remarkably, whatever is happening, there is always a silver lining. It might take time to actually discover what that might be.

This is an extension of being positive, but it takes things to a whole new level.

Someone I know learned the hard way that having a credit card was dangerous. They discovered that they were far more responsible when they used cash or a debit card. That way they could watch their balance decrease. Scary, yet the silver lining is that they learned early in life that you can go into debt quickly if you're not paying attention - and not to do that anymore.

Years ago, I injured my back. I discovered when I went dancing that if I told a heavy-handed dance partner about my pain, he was much gentler. After that, when he asked me how my back was doing, I realized that if I told him that I was still in pain our partnership was much more comfortable. (I'm embarrassed to admit that I kept saying my back still hurt once I was fully healed but it worked!)

So getting injured produced a positive outcome that I certainly would never have predicted in advance.

Silver linings - they can stun
If only we dare look for one.

So often we are in our head
Or saddened, we run to our bed.

But take a chance and you might see
One hiding now behind that tree!

Oh, there it is - it waits for me
Truly a gift I did not originally see.

Though now I like and often find
The positive I'd previously leave behind.

\- Karen Leeds

SECRET #22: PROCESS EMOTIONS TO RELEASE THEM

(They won't be lonely - I bet someone else will grab them.)

Years ago, a marriage counselor* suggested that it is important to process emotions that you feel. Otherwise, they become trapped in your body for years. She said if you hide something under the rug, you'll trip over it later.

Most of us don't realize how much our feelings might hold us back and interfere in relationships. We bite our tongues when it would be better to say what is on our minds. We give our subconscious power to run our lives! Forgiving yourself and others allows you to move on. (We can forgive without forgetting what happened.)

One way to release feelings is to write letters

THAT YOU DON'T SEND!**

These letters can be to yourself or others (alive or not). Don't worry about sentence structure, grammar, or anything else. It is a way to put everything out there so that YOU no longer have the burden of carrying it with you wherever you go - like a huge unwanted suitcase or backpack. Life will feel much easier.

When you're upset, try punching pillows instead of walls. Maybe when you're alone? (Don't scare pets or humans.)

* Dr. Ronni Michaelson
** Landmark Education courses suggest writing letters. (Legal says we can't be held responsible if you mail these and upset others. They are for you to process feelings.)

Those strong emotions - let them go
The world doesn't always have to know.

How sad you've been, angry or afraid
Your feelings ruled and this bed you made.

But you can change it - that is true
It all comes simply down to you.

So, grab that pillow, don't punch a wall
It's time now - so stop your stall.

End lashing out at an innocent other
And give up trying to emotion smother.

Feel those feelings and remember to breathe
It's healthier than when you start to seethe.

Your time is here so take a stand
And others can help give you a hand.

Your life awaits - how peaceful it can be
Just take a chance and soon you'll see.

So, wave goodbye to feelings gone
Thank goodness you can now go on!

\- Karen Leeds

SECRET #23: WRITE WHAT YOU WANT TO HAPPEN

(You're like a genie granting yourself a wish.)

You can choose to live an amazing life.

Picture what you want to happen! Then write it down as if it already happened and establish a deadline for accomplishing it. And write it down 10 times! (Creating a timeline is helpful here so it will feel tangible and real.)

You decide WHAT you want and by WHEN. You can leave it up to the universe to decide HOW it will happen. Isn't it nice that you don't have to worry about the details of bringing it to fruition?

You get to play a huge role in shaping your life. I termed this the Playdoh Principle - shaping your life the way you want it to be as if you were using Playdoh. Wouldn't it be nice if changing your life were that easy? It can be!

For example, I might say:

I have published my third book by January 2023.

What do you want? And if you feel uncomfortable asking - that's okay. You're allowed to put it out there. Go for it! By the way, the more you do things like this, the easier you will find it to do so. (Yikes - off to finish that book!)

What is it that you really want?
Come on now, find a pen or font.

It might be scary but take a chance
And with this life you'll learn to dance.

Open up and write it down
And then go skip about the town.

Your dreams will soon come true for you
But only if you choose what and who

And when and where and so much more
Just look at the excitement you have in store.

The world will open up to you
When energy flows - strong and true.

Your fate is cemented - feeling alive
I see you there starting to thrive.

- Karen Leeds

SECRET #24: LOVE YOURSELF WITHOUT RESERVATION

(Let go now - admit you're awesome. I won't tell - or maybe I will!)

It is hard for some of us to fully love ourselves. It might be the result of things that happened with parents, other kids, teachers or bosses. (My scary 10th grade biology presentation didn't help me to feel good about myself.)

Try this wonderful exercise - circulating for decades:

Say "I LOVE YOU" into the mirror. And say it 10 times!

Some people struggle with this. If you have difficulty doing so, try a sentence that you might feel more comfortable saying like "I am beginning to love myself."

It is important to believe that you are loved - especially by yourself. That way you are on your own side. This is critical because then you will be able to take any action knowing that your subconscious won't sabotage you.

And if you find that you can't fully love yourself yet, I'll believe in and hold space for you until you can.

I LOVE YOU! Yep - you. That's right. You are awesome just as you are. Frankly, I have always felt that way!

(It took decades to say I love my quirky sense of humor.)

No matter who took love away
Or made you sad - for a year or a day.

Just give love back to yourself right now
Stand before the mirror - you'll see how.

The person looking back at you
Sees you are great - don't wince, it's true.

Now there - I see you've shown your grin
That's what we want - it helps you win.

For all those who said you're dumb or bad
Shake that away - now don't be sad.

You don't need those who took you down
Give up that semi-permanent frown.

Caused by all who made you feel small
Look, now you can suddenly stand so tall.

Now you are here supporting you
There - that's the way - you can love yourself too!

- Karen Leeds

SECRET #25: ENVISION YOUR VISION

(Hey - I just enjoy saying that since it rhymes.)

Close your eyes and imagine that what you want to bring about has come true.

Can you see it? Try filling in the details to make it tangible and specific.

The more concrete and detailed, the more likely you can see it and keep it in your mind.

NAME IT!

Let's say I'm imagining publishing my 3rd book by January, 2023. I see myself at the library giving a talk with a stack of books for people who want to buy a copy. Which room at the library am I in? What outfit am I wearing? I picture the smile on my face. I also notice who is there - whether adults or teenagers. How are they responding? Are they nodding? Asking questions?

Details help it to feel much more tangible.

Most importantly, it helps your subconscious discover what you are looking to create; almost like a blueprint for a house that an architect/you design for the builder/your subconscious. Then let your subconscious take the wheel!

Envision your vision - hey that's fun to say!
It can be yours - let's picture that day.

You see it now in all its glory
And flush out details for your story.

You get to have it all I bet
Though you may not quite see it yet.

Your life will slowly start to change
That future will soon come into range.

It's bound to happen - just declare it
And have the guts to see - I dare it.

So now trek onward - there's no wall
It's your turn - fate - to have it all!

- Karen Leeds

SECRET #26: YOU DID A GOOD JOB!

(Hey - maybe give yourself a treat? You deserve it!)

This is a powerful exercise - and one of my favorites.

Write down 10 things that you want to congratulate yourself for doing during the day.

Writing these at night before bed is great timing. (If I'm really excited about something I did I will write it down then, instead of waiting for bedtime.)

It is a terrific way to motivate yourself to regularly do things that lift you up.

Bonus points for items like speaking up and setting boundaries. When you reward yourself for doing things like that, you encourage yourself to do them again.

Years ago, I had odd symptoms, so a friend suggested I see a rheumatologist. I asked my doctor, but she said that she had done all the rheumatological tests.

I gathered my courage and said:

> "I don't mean to be disrespectful, but if you could
> do all the rheumatological tests, why would there be
> a branch of medicine called rheumatology?"

My doctor wrote me a referral, and remarkably I got diagnosed and treated!

Today I again wrote down those ten
And that great feeling built again.

Can't wait to record what I do
And share with me (not so much with you).

I feel both capable and strong
This muscle built - it didn't take long.

But here it is, and I am impressed
I did so much more than getting dressed.

At times I run to write what I did
With pen in hand - so the wins haven't hid.

I feel accomplished though this took awhile
And now I like my new winning style.

It builds me up and lets me know
That I'm the one who's running this show!

- Karen Leeds

SECRET #27: FEEL GRATEFUL

(There's got to be something. It will come to you - I think.)

Write down three things you are grateful for each day.

This puts you in a state of gratitude and is helpful in the way you show up in your life.

I decided to try to make these three things unique so that I wasn't recording the same things every day. Sure, I'm grateful for my kids, the weather, and having savings in the bank. But I thought it might be helpful to get creative and be very specific and detailed.

Example: My neighbor asked if I would take care of her cat while she was away on vacation. I was nervous since I knew little about cats but by the end of the week the cat and I had bonded so completely that she would try to sneak out the door with me when I left. What a surprise!

Example: I miss my dad who died years ago. But one day I realized I have his rock and shell collection. I had never done anything with it; those I'd gotten had sat in a glass case. So I took out my favorite pieces and found a wooden frame to display them on my wall. I love seeing them because not only are they beautiful, but they are a constant reminder of him. (I have books he has written but those sit in the study on a shelf and don't make me smile.)

Unless we write down what we like
Those thoughts might suddenly take a hike.

Amazing things happen every day
And gratitude keeps them coming our way.

A dog I don't know came up to me
And placed its paw upon my knee.

A stranger I helped cried tears of joy
At my kindness -- it was not a ploy.

I was sick for two weeks but now am good
My health came back as I believed it would.

An incredible sunset -- I see it now
I feel so honored to notice that -- wow.

Sure, life at times can be stressful that's true
But ponder things and see them anew!

- Karen Leeds

SECRET #28: MAKE YOUR DESIRE TANGIBLE

(Seeing it makes such a difference.)

You've probably heard about making a vision board using magazines.

You can get creative: cut out words or letters, find fabrics and other decorations.

Choose pictures of people, nature, scenery, and animals. There are no hard and fast rules. It is best if you go for things that seem to resonate with you and truly capture the feeling you want to achieve.

What is interesting is that you are actually communicating with your subconscious. Most of us don't realize that our subconscious is really driving 90% of what happens in our lives! So if you display detailed images that your subconscious sees regularly, it might say "Oh, now I get it - that's what you want." And the universe takes up your cause as well.

I have heard of people putting a picture of a house on a vision board and they end up moving into that very same house! So these things really do make a difference.

(Note: Legal is making me say that we can't guarantee the same will happen with your vision board - but don't let that stop you. Maybe you'll get the house next door to it!)

When you make a vision board - it's there
For you and your subconscious - the two can share.

You'll see what you want right now and be happy
Suddenly it feels real - sure, go and get sappy.

As if your dream walked into your life
Maybe a job, a new friend, a trip, or a wife.

Fantasy seems real and how great is that?
Your heart is full instead of pancake flat.

Your subconscious now gets what you want to be
And soon it is yours - quite consciously.

Your destiny will unfold as it's meant to do
Making your life now work very well for you!

- Karen Leeds

SECRET #29: GIVE YOURSELF PERMISSION TO BE DIFFERENT

(Knock yourself out - hey not literally. You okay there?)

You don't need to be predictable.

I remember years ago a CEO explained that he had to leave early. We all assumed that he was going to an important meeting but then it occurred to me that he could be leaving early for the weekend. Or going to watch his kid's baseball game. Who knew why he left?

I talked with a woman awhile back. She explained that she used the fact that she was blonde to her advantage. When someone asked her a question that she didn't want to answer, she would shrug her shoulders or shake her head and smile like she didn't get it. What a clever idea!

You are not required to answer a question or explain yourself. Most people won't call you out on it and demand an answer.

> (And frankly, if they do, maybe that's not someone with whom you would prefer to hang out?)

My daughter came home from a wedding shower with a sparkly hat. I have a stuffed llama and I discovered that the llama wanted to wear the hat.

> (I'm partly teasing here - but if people wonder about my hat-wearing llama, that's okay. I'm not on earth to be predictable and always rational - at least about things that aren't truly important.)

You're allowed to be who you are meant to be
Go for it - and you'll start to see.

Unique or odd - it doesn't matter
The world will love you - (be a mad hatter).

You find that you're suddenly feeling so free
To be yourself - (not like the others or me).

Truly you - now take a stand
You can be the best you - here in the land.

You now have such energy and more
You stopped pushing yourself down as you did before.

Such a feeling of freedom can be quite heady
Enjoy yourself - feeling incredibly steady.

Powerful beyond what you possibly thought
Stop being the "you" others believed that you ought.

\- Karen Leeds

SECRET #30: GET OUT OF YOUR COMFORT ZONE

(I get it - wait that looks really comfy!)

We often get stuck in our comfort zone doing what we have predictably done for years. But we don't need to stay there - at least for things that aren't important. (Choosing to pay taxes is probably still a good idea though.)

What if you occasionally do the opposite of what people expect?

I went to an animal show-and-tell. They asked if someone wanted to hold a baby fox. I remember thinking "Too bad that's not something I would typically volunteer to do."

But then I thought, why not? That baby fox was cute. So I raised my hand and got to hold this adorable creature. (Granted they did suggest I not get it too close to my nose because it might think it was a nut and bite it - yikes!)

One day my GPS said to turn right four times and then turn left. I was going to turn left initially. I knew it!

Another time I programmed my GPS. It suggested a certain route. I thought there was a faster way to get there so I went the way I thought made sense and saved 20 minutes; puzzling. I sometimes find the GPS voice is a bit parental and bossy. (Wait, she didn't hear me, did she?)

It's okay - you can be who you are
Whatever that is - in your life you're the star.

Try new things out of your comfort zone
Feel free to travel or even to roam.

Predictability can be quite boring
The last thing we want is to have ourselves snoring.

So, find yourself and how you see you
Feel free to experiment - many tried this, too.

Take yourself out of that boring rut
And maybe soon you'll start to strut.

That's the way you can grow (I knew it)
There's really not that much more to it.

You're allowed to change and get out of your box
Suddenly that life of yours now rocks!

\- Karen Leeds

SUMMARY OF 20 SECRETS

You Only Understand (what works for you)
True Strength and Bravery (being authentic)
Stop Trying to be Perfect (we're human and that's ok)
The Magic of Possibility (believe)
Tune in To What You Want (pay attention)
Don't Throw Yourself Under a Bus (stop overserving)
Create Momentum (small changes to start)
Don't Take Rejection Personally (it's not about you)
When to Toss the Plan (if it isn't working for you)
Be Strong and Confident (believe in yourself)
You Are Loved, Worthy and Enough (we all are)
The Mind is a Scary Place (don't venture there alone)
Watch Your Language (notice what you say out loud)
What Would You Do If You Won (what would bring joy)
Live in the Present (don't give in to worry or guilt)
How Do You Spend Your Time (what are you doing)
Interruptions (might not need to drop everything)
Decision-Making (heart vs. head decisions)
Up Until Now (draw a line in the sand - you can change)
Power of Positivity (it makes a difference)

SUMMARY OF 10 SUBCONSCIOUS/ UNIVERSE SECRETS

Look for the Silver Lining (there is always one)
Process Emotions to Release Them (let feelings go)
What You Want to Happen (what is your goal)
Love Yourself Without Reservation (embrace yourself)
Envision Your Vision (picture what you want)
You Did a Good Job (pat yourself on the back)
Feel Grateful (notice the things that are going well)
Make Your Desire Tangible (see the specific details)
Give Yourself Permission to be Different (quirky is fine)
Get Out of Your Comfort Zone (try something new)

To Schedule a 60 Minute 1:1 Coaching Session, Contact

Karen@LifeCoachingMagic.com

with COACHING in subject line

Bring your dreams to earth while you are still here to enjoy them!

SPEAK SO PEOPLE HEAR YOU

7 Ways in Which People are Different that Matter to Relationships

14 Little-Known Communication Secrets

Made in the USA
Middletown, DE
05 February 2023

23521415R00046